Tow your Fifth Wheel Trailer Like a Pro

A complete guide to professional driving techniques for beginners to experienced drivers

LORRIN WALSH

Drive Smart Publications

Printed by Gorham Printing, U.S.A.

ISBN10: 0-9785788-2-1
ISBN13: 978-0-9785788-2-4

CONTENTS

PREFACE

When most people learn to drive they are just taught the *hows* and not the *whys*. Teaching the whys, or the mechanics, of driving gives people the tools and skills they can apply to any vehicle or situation.

INTRODUCTION

I know what your first two questions are going to be: "Who is this guy?" and, "How does he know this stuff?"

After more than 30 years of experience driving RVs, I considered myself a skilled driver. Then, about 10 years ago, I went to work for Gray Line of Seattle. As I went through their training course I realized how much I knew... how much I knew, but didn't understand... and how much I didn't know.

When driving a larger vehicle, such as a motor coach, or when pulling a trailer, the larger size and weight make the driving and maneuvering that you routinely do in your car feel totally different.

Currently I am a Driver/Guide. In the past I was a driving instructor for Gray Line of Seattle. As an instructor I trained people to drive motor coaches from 20 feet in length up to 60-foot articulated ones with rear steering. One of the things I notice when instructing is that while the students know how to drive, they generally don't understand the mechanics of driving.

I know what you are thinking: "How can a guy who teaches tour-coach driving know anything about pulling trailers?"

Well, driving is 90 percent mental and only 10 percent physical. And, while the physics of maneuvering are a little bit more complicated when you add a trailer, the same principals still apply.

I started pulling travel trailers when I was driving with a

Learner's Permit. My parents had trailers for many years and our first RV was a travel trailer. I later migrated to motorhomes, but still pull trailers for pleasure and sometimes for work.

When you drive you probably use reference points to help guide you. One of the problems I've encountered as an instructor is that people were taught to drive by reference points, but they were not taught how the reference points were established.

For example, I had a student who had been driving city and school buses. She was a good driver. In her previous training she was taught how to make maneuvers, but not the technical aspects of doing so. She was taught things such as: "turn when the curb reaches the second window post" but not *why* she needed to wait. I call this "reference point" driving. After two days on a skills' course, she came to me and said she had thought she knew how to drive, but now realized she didn't.

After a while you will start making maneuvers based on reference points, which is not a bad thing. But because the reference points will be different for each vehicle, I believe in teaching the rules so that you will understand *why* you need to perform a specific action. By understanding the rules, you can apply them to anything you drive.

I believe the information provided in this book will prove to be as useful to the experienced driver as it is to the novice. Sometimes the simplest thing will trigger that "AHA!" moment, which ultimately helps you understand why you do something, or why you need to do something.

CHAPTER 1

Before You Start

Stuff, but very important stuff

Selecting a Vehicle

If you already have a truck and fifth wheel trailer it's good to go back and review the weights, by axle. Over time, you may have added things that could affect the various load ratings. You have the advantage of being able to weigh your rigs and compare them to the truck and trailer's ratings.

If you don't already own a fifth wheel trailer or truck, this is where you should start. A good understanding of the basics will help you make the right choices when selecting a trailer and tow vehicle.

There are many things that should be considered when buying and towing a fifth wheel trailer. For instance: How large a trailer do you want? What size truck do you need? Or, if you already have one, will the truck you have be sufficient to handle the trailer you're considering?

Let's start by going over some of the terms and definitions you will need to know before you can make any final decisions:

Gross Vehicle Weight Rating (GVWR): The maximum permissible weight of the vehicle, truck or trailer. This includes all personal items, cargo, fluids, any options/ accessories installed, as well as passengers.

Gross Vehicle Weight (GVW): The actual weight of the truck. To find out this weight take your vehicle to a public scale and have it weighed. You should weigh each axle to make sure you are also within the axle limits.

Curb Weight (CW): The weight of the truck that includes all fluids and fuel but does not include any passengers, options, aftermarket installed equipment, or cargo.

Gross Trailer Weight (GTW): The actual weight of the trailer. Similar to the GVW, except it is the scaled weight of the trailer. This includes the axle weight and the hitch weight.

Unloaded Vehicle Weight (UVW): Commonly referred to as "Dry Weight," this is the weight you will generally find used in trailer brochures. It is the weight of the trailer, as built at the factory, and does not include any options, aftermarket accessories, LP gas or water.

Gross Axle Weight Rating (GAWR): The maximum allowed weight for each axle. Vehicles are designed as a unit; if you take the rating for each axle and add them up together, it can be greater that the GVWR.

Cargo Carrying Capacity (CCC): The maximum weight of all personal items, any options/accessories installed, and cargo that can be carried by the vehicle.

Net Payload (NP): The weight that can be placed on the truck. This does not include the weight of the driver, passengers, options, or aftermarket accessories.

Maximum Payload (MP): The maximum weight that the truck is designed to carry. It includes all passengers, options, aftermarket accessories, and cargo.

Gross Combined Weight Rating (GCWR): The maximum permissible weight of the truck and trailer combined when both are fully loaded for travel.

Gross Combined Weight (GCW): The actual combined weight of the truck and trailer, both loaded for travel.

Hitch Weight (HW): Sometimes called "Kingpin" weight, this is the weight of the trailer pressing down on the truck. This should be 15 to 25 percent of the loaded weight for a fifth wheel trailer. Some people will refer to this as Tongue Weight (TW), which is a carry-over from conventional trailers.

Maximum Loaded Trailer Weight Rating (MLTWR): The maximum loaded trailer weight that the truck is designed to tow. This allowable weight for a fifth wheel trailer can be different than that for a conventional trailer.

Understanding this information at the beginning will be helpful when selecting your vehicles. If you currently do not have a truck or trailer, start by choosing the trailer of your dreams. Get all the information you can about the trailer, the Gross Vehicle Weight Rating, Unloaded Vehicle Weight, Hitch Weight, etc. See if the manufacturer has provided any additional information stating how much each factory-installed option weighs.

Manufacturers that are members of the Recreation Vehicle Industry Association (RVIA) will have installed an additional sticker on the back of a closet or cabinet door with this information. Keep in mind that the weight of everything that is added to the basic vehicle will be deducted from the Cargo Carrying Capacity.

With your trailer you will have the Unloaded Vehicle Weight, plus any installed options, as well as whatever you're going to put in the trailer to establish the actual weight. Unless you have years of experience weighing rigs empty and full to monitor how much added load you may carry, my recommendation is to use the Gross Vehicle Weight Rating of the trailer when you are selecting a tow vehicle.

I would also use 25 percent of the Gross Vehicle Weight Rating for the Hitch Weight. This gives you a little growing room and an extra margin of safety. If you already have a trailer, go weigh it, and use that information.

Sample Trailer Information:

7,492	GVWR
6,158	UVW
1,367	HW (from manufacture)
1,873	HW (25 percent of GVWR)

Once you have gathered all the information on the fifth wheel trailer you can start planning what type of truck you will need to pull it.

As you look through the truck specifications you will be bombarded with all sorts of charts and tables listing engines, transmissions and axle ratios, as well as different body configurations, each with their own ratings. It is easy to just pick a number that matches your trailer weight and believe that this will work.

The problem is that things are designed to work as a unit and the sum of the maximum rating for each part can, and usually does, far exceed the overall combined rating—the Gross Combined Weight Rating.

I am sure that you already have a specific tow vehicle in mind, but before you choose your preferred style/type of truck, you need to establish which one has a towing capacity that will handle the trailer you want. If you pick a truck first, before you run the numbers, it's easy to get caught up in the moment and overlook something that could be a problem later.

No matter which truck you choose some things will remain the same. The next step in the process is to estimate the load you expect your truck to carry. This would include passengers and miscellaneous items, such as tools, chains, emergency equipment, the fifth wheel hitch, and the estimated hitch weight of the trailer.

Estimated Truck Net Payload:

330	Passengers
225	Cargo
150	Hitch
+ 1,873	Hitch Weight
2,578	Total Estimated Net Payload

This estimated weight does not include things such as factory-installed options, or dealer-installed accessories. These will vary by vehicle and will be factored in later in the calculations.

Start your selection process by taking your total estimated net payload and look for a truck that has a payload capacity greater than your estimate. And a Maximum Loaded Trailer Weight Rating greater than the trailer you have selected. After you have found a truck that has the capacity, also record its Gross Vehicle Weight Rating and Gross Combined Weight Rating.

Truck Data:

3,030	Maximum Payload
11,300	Maximum Loaded Trailer Weight Rating
8,200	Gross Vehicle Weight Rating
16,700	Gross Combined Weight Rating

Next, find the Curb Weight of the truck. Do a rough calculation by taking the Gross Vehicle Weight Rating and subtracting the Maximum Payload.

Calculated Curb Weight:

8,200	Gross Vehicle Weight Rating
- 3,030	Maximum Payload
5,170	Estimated Curb Weight

The next step is to take the Curb Weight and add your estimated Net Payload, factory-installed options, and dealer-installed accessories. Don't overlook the little things, they all add up. For example, a spray-in bed-liner can add up to 50 pounds; those oversize tires and fancy wheels, another 150 pounds.

Calculated Gross Vehicle Weight:

5,170	Curb Weight
2,578	Total estimated Net Payload
150	Factory-installed Options
+ 300	Dealer-installed or after market accessories
8,198	Estimated Gross Vehicle Weight

The last step is to subtract the Hitch Weight from the Gross Vehicle Weight to get the Net Gross Vehicle Weight. If you do not subtract the Hitch Weight you would be counting it twice in the calculations. Then, add the Net Gross Vehicle Weight and the trailer Gross Vehicle Weight Rating and you will come up with the Gross Combined Weight.

Final Calculation:

8,198	Gross Vehicle Weight
- 1,873	Hitch Weight
= 6,325	Net Gross Vehicle Weight
+ 7,492	Trailer Gross Vehicle Weight Rating
=13,817	Gross Combined Weight

Based on this Gross Combined Weight Rating the truck is capable of doing the job because it is less than the 16,700 pounds Gross Combined Weight Rating. The problem I have with this truck is that it has a Gross Vehicle Weight of 8,198 pounds, but the Gross Vehicle Weight Rating is 8,200 pounds. This only leaves a safety margin of 2 pounds.

The truck's maximum trailer rating was good—11,300 pounds versus the trailer's Gross Vehicle Weight Rating of 7,492 pounds. I also realize that I used the Gross Vehicle Weight Rating of the trailer for the calculations. Even if you reduced the load in the trailer by 1,000 pounds that would only reduce the hitch weight by about 250… which would give a larger overall margin but the truck load would still be close to the Gross Vehicle Weight Rating. Being this close to the limit would not allow for the reserve capacity to haul those extra passengers (or those perfect garden statues you just had to buy for your home).

My recommendation here would be to move up to a truck with a higher Gross Vehicle Weight Rating. Also, if you are like most people, and if this is your first RV, in about 2-3 years you will be looking for a larger trailer and the truck would not be able to handle the larger trailer.

If you already have a truck, just reverse the process. The best thing to do is load your truck with people, cargo, etc., weigh it, and don't forget to add the Hitch Weight of the trailer. Having an actual weight eliminates some of the guesswork. Take your actual weight from the Gross Combined Weight Rating, and then use either that number or the Maximum Towing Capacity—whichever number is smaller—to determine what trailer your truck can accommodate.

After you have done all your calculations and found the right rig, do an axle-by-axle double-check to ensure that each axle is adequate to handle the load.

The tires that come with a new truck are matched to the rated axle load. On a used truck, if the tires have been replaced, you should check the load-carrying capacity to ensure they are adequate.

I have included a work sheet in an Appendix to help you gather data and work out your own calculations.

Hitches

After you select the truck of your needs you will have to see what type of hitch meets your requirements. Because of the variety of trucks and how you want to use the truck when not towing a trailer, there is a range of hitches available to include: Fixed, Air-ride, Sliding, and Goose Neck.

The standard pick-up box is eight-feet-long. Anything less than that is considered a short bed. When properly installed, the center of the hitch will be just ahead of the rear axle. For a short bed pick-up you need to use a pin box extension or a sliding hitch assembly to allow more clearance when maneuvering in tight situations. **Note**: Before you add a pin box extension check with the trailer manufacturer for any restrictions that may apply.

A sliding hitch assembly has two positions. One is for traveling on the road where it is locked just ahead of the rear axle; the second where it is unlocked and the trailer is allowed to slide back towards the tailgate. Different manufacturers have several variations on this type of system. This gives you more room between the trailer and the cab, reducing the chance of damaging the rear of the cab or rear window while turning.

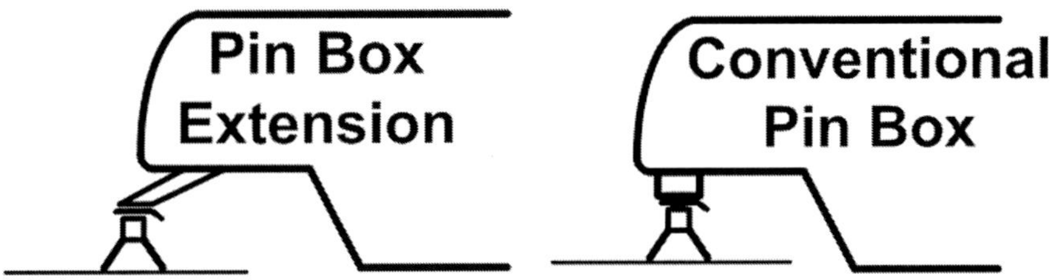

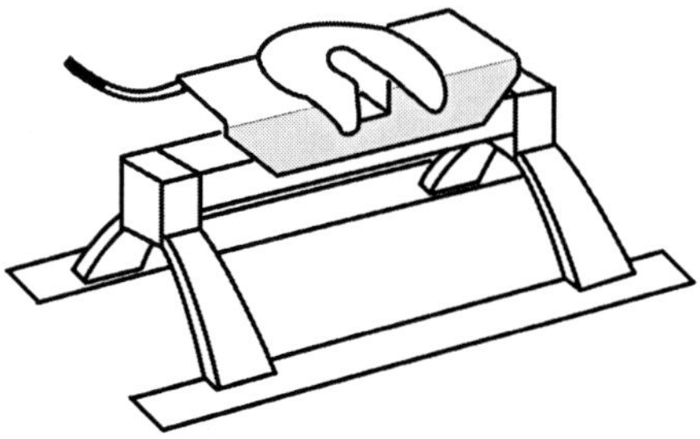

Fifth wheel hitch assembly

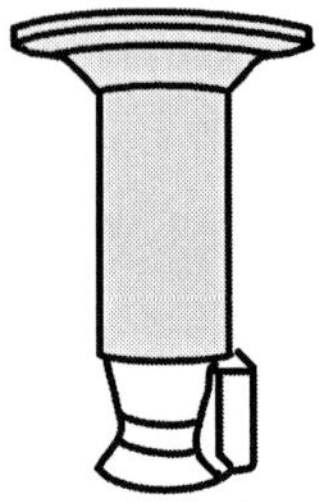

Goose neck adapter

There are also hitches for fifth wheel trailers that are called Goose Neck hitches. These differ in that they use a ball for the connection, rather than a fifth wheel plate. The ball is mounted in the bed of the truck. In some installations the support structure is mounted below the bed so the ball can be removed, and a cover plate installed, which leaves the bed clear when you want to use the pick-up for other things. There are adapters available to convert most fifth wheel hitch trailers to a Goose Neck configuration. Again, check with the trailer manufacturer to see if there are any restrictions for using a Goose Neck adaptor.

Drive smart by selecting the right combination

CHAPTER 2

Getting Ready

Where do I start?

The first thing you do when getting ready for any trip is to get into your tow vehicle and sit down. So let's start here.

Seat Position

Positioning the seat properly is a subject I think people really do not understand. The first thing is to use good posture and sit up straight—just like your mother told you to do!

If your seat has a height or tilt adjustment feature, position it so that there is a slight space between the lower portion of your upper leg (just above the knee) and the seat. This space is helpful as it aids circulation. Reduced circulation in your legs can cause fatigue and cramps. If your seat has no height adjustment, consider raising the floor level by making a small platform.

Hitching Up a Fifth Wheel Trailer

Before starting to hitch up make sure that the trailer is securely chocked so that it will not move accidently.

1. Remove/retract any stabilization supports.
2. Position the king pin on the trailer so it is at, or slightly below, the height of the coupler using the trailer jacks.
3. Drop the tailgate.
4. Ensure the coupler lock bar is open to allow the king pin to engage the jaws on the hitch plate.
5. Slowly back up until the king pin engages the coupler jaws. This step is much easier if you have an assistant to adjust the height of the trailer as necessary when you are backing into the hitch.
6. Engage the coupler-locking bar and set the safety latch.
7. Close the tailgate.
8. Connect the light and brake electrical cable, and secure the break-away safety cable to a secure attachment point.
9. Slightly raise the jacks off the ground and do a gentle pull test to be sure the trailer is secure and the coupler is latched.
10. Raise the jacks completely, then raise and securely stow the landing gear.
11. Make sure all services are disconnected.
12. Remove wheel chocks.

Before you start to move do a complete pre-trip inspection (detailed later in this chapter).

The procedure for unhitching a fifth wheel trailer is basically the reverse of hitching, but is still worth going over.

1. After you pull into the site where you are going to unhitch from the trailer and you complete any blocking under the wheels for leveling, securely chock the wheels so the trailer will not move.
2. Drop and secure the fifth wheel landing gear first, then use the jacks to raise the trailer to unload (remove the weight from) the hitch.
3. Disconnect the light and brake electrical cable, as well as the break-away safety cable. Stow them so they will not get tangled when unhitching the truck.
4. Drop the tailgate.
5. After ensuring that the parking brake of your tow vehicle is securely set, disengage the locking bar safety latch and open the locking bar. If it does not want to open you will need to move the tow vehicle very gently by releasing the parking brake, putting the transmission in gear—usually the opposite from the way you were last moving—and do not apply any fuel/acceleration, to relieve the pressure on the latch pin. Remember, before you get out of the seat reset the parking brake and put the transmission out of gear. If you have an assistant they can open the lock bar when it becomes free and adjust the height of the trailer as necessary.
6. Slowly drive out from under the trailer, ensuring that you do not snag any of the cables.
7. Raise the tailgate.
8. Complete leveling and site connections.

What can happen if you do not properly chock the trailer and/or secure the landing gear.

Pre-Trip inspection

As a commercial driver, I am required to perform an extensive list of inspections and document them on a Vehicle Inspection Report before I start every trip. There are all sorts of lists out there on what to check before starting. If you follow one of them, good for you. If you don't, I would recommend the checklist below as a minimum:

1. Do a basic leak check. Are there any puddles or streams running out from under your tow vehicle?
2. Check basic fluid levels, oil and water.
3. Start the engine and check the instruments. Do you have oil pressure? Is the electrical system charging? If the engine does not start right away it's better to let the engine crank for a while (i.e. 30 seconds) rather than using short bursts of the starter. This is especially important for diesel engines. The highest battery draw is when you start to turn the engine over. Once you get the engine rolling the starter draws a lot less current.

4. Check your tires. The best way is to use a pressure gage, but at a minimum "thump" them. Use a steel bar or hardwood stick and hit the tread face of the tire, not the corner or side. This gives you the best indication. A properly inflated tire will have a ringing sound, while a flat tire just thuds. After a while you will even be able to tell when a tire's pressure is low. I use a pressure gage before each trip and then periodically during the trip to ensure that the tires are at the manufacturer's recommended pressure for the load being carried.

   Check the face of the tires to see how they are wearing. Are they cupping or scrubbing? That could indicate an alignment problem. It's better to find out early that you have a problem before you ruin a tire.

   If you have a remote pressure monitoring system you may be thinking: "I don't need to do this step." Even though the remote systems are nice, they do not tell you the physical condition of the tire.

   If possible, also check the lug nuts to see if any are loose. Ideally you would check the lug nut torque with a torque wrench. Checking the lug nuts by trying to turn each one by hand is a good basic check. If you see rust trails from any of the lugs, even if they are tight, have them checked as it could indicate a problem.

   Also don't forget to check your spare tires once in a while.

   While I'm on the subject of tires, let's talk about flats. If you have a flat outside dual tire, you can drive at slow speed for a reasonable distance to get to a safe location. If you have an inside dual flat, don't move the rig at all. A flat inside dual can damage the brake lines.

5. Check *all* your lights, including the four-way flashers.
6. Check the hitch coupler lock and safety latch.
7. Check the electrical connection and breakaway cable.
8. Since you are walking around your rig anyway, checking tires and lights, it might be a good time to check the following:
   - Is the landing gear up and stowed / jacks up?
   - Is the antenna down?
   - Are all the compartment doors closed and latched?
   - Have you removed all the wheel covers and chocks?
   - Are all the services (power, water, cable) disconnected?
   - Are there any unusual sounds?
9. Don't forget to also check the inside of your rig.
   - Is everything stowed?
   - Refrigerator door latched?

When you stop for a break during the day, take a minute to do a mid-trip inspection, a basic observation check. Walk around to check the tires and general conditions.

When I stop for a break I take my tire thumper and walk around the rig and check the tires. I also feel each tire with the back of my hand to check temperature. I have heard about people who recommend using infrared temperature sensors to measure tire temperatures. My response to that is: there's nothing wrong with doing it that way, and if you want to do that, knock yourself out… but don't "techno" yourself to death. When you stop and find one tire a few degrees warmer than another it may be nothing more than an uneven road surface that has put a little more load on one tire or the other. When driving on roads that have ruts from 18-wheelers your track width is slightly different so your tires get uneven loading, which will cause uneven temperatures. It could also be as simple as one side of your rig having been in the sun all day. Don't chase something that you can't do much about. The back of the hand will give you a good general indication of how things are doing. (The back of the hand is more sensitive than the front, which has built up calluses over time that reduces sensitivity.)

The bottom line when you are checking pressures and temperatures is: "The more accurate the measuring instrument, the more unobtainable the goal."

At the end of the day do a post-trip inspection. Walk-around just like the pre-trip inspection. It is better to discover a problem at the end of the day so you have time to take care of it, rather than in the morning when you are trying to get underway.

Setting Mirrors

Proper mirror setting is one of the most important aspects of getting ready. Approximately 30 percent of the hazards you will encounter come from the rear, so getting the maximum viewing area from your mirrors is critical.

And, just like for any vehicle, you need to know where the Pivot Point is for your trailer. So properly adjusting your mirrors, and then establishing where you see the Pivot Point in the mirrors, is important. I will cover how to identify where your trailer's Pivot Point is in Chapter 3.

The standard mirrors on most pickups are usually insufficient for towing a trailer.

A standard mirror generally does not extend beyond the outside edge of the trailer. If you look at the following sketch you will see that this situation creates a blind spot, which, at the back of the trailer, can be 4-5 feet wide.

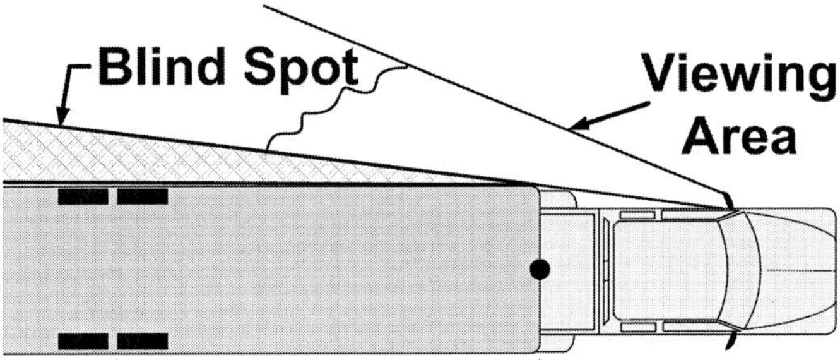

When you are towing a trailer your mirrors need to be extended so that when you stand in front of your rig and sight down the sides, the inside edge of the mirror is flush with the outside edge of the trailer on the driver's side, and flush with the awning arm, if you have one, or the side of the trailer on the passenger side.

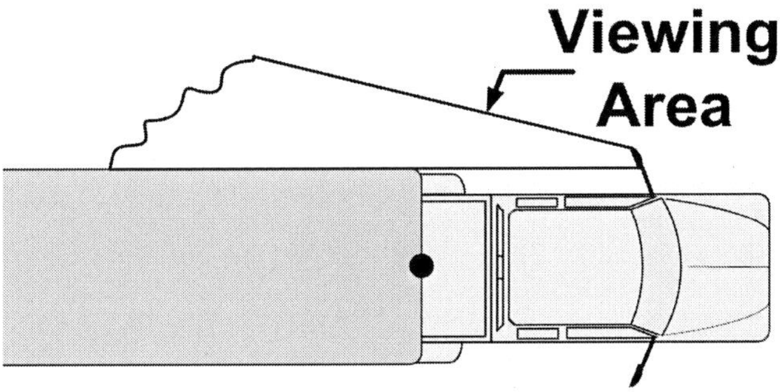

You may not think that it is possible to set a mirror too far out, but it is. Although yes, the farther out you set a mirror the more you will be able to see behind the trailer… At the same time you are losing valuable viewing area to the outside.

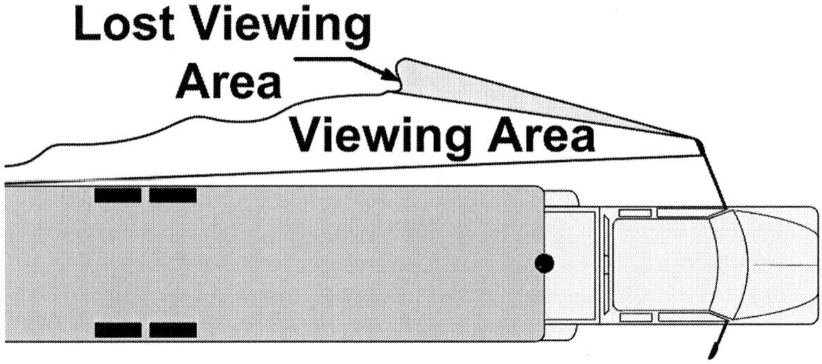

I know you are thinking that this is a little bit exaggerated, and I did it to show what happens. But, believe me, I have seen worse.

The view is free—use it, do not waste it.

Now adjust the flat part of the mirror so you can just see the side of your trailer along the inside edge of the mirror. Set it with as little view of the trailer as you are comfortable with. You also want to be looking back level with the ground between a quarter and a third of the way from the top of the mirror. You really don't need to see a lot of sky, unless you are driving on a runway.

If the convex (a.k.a. "spot") mirrors are independently adjustable, set them the best that you can so that you can see out horizontally to the ground and alongside the trailer. Most people do not use their convex mirrors for general driving because it's not easy to see any detail. You may not see the detail, but the fact that you are seeing a much larger area gives you an advantage.

Think of your convex/spot mirrors as an early warning device. They warn you of a developing situation in order for you to take necessary action. It may take several seconds for what you see in your convex mirror to show up in the flat mirror, if it ever does. I will talk about what to do with that extra time later in Chapter 7. When set properly the convex mirrors should be used as much as the flat mirrors for general driving. Sometimes, when training drivers, we will cover up the flat mirrors to force them to learn how to drive using the spot mirrors. If you don't have independently adjustable convex mirrors, consider installing some. There are many types and kits available.

Overall Dimensions

It's a good idea to know the overall dimensions of your rig before you come to that low overpass and it's too late.

You should measure your hard and soft clearances as well as width. Hard clearance is the height of the tallest hard object on the roof, like the A/C or satellite dome. The soft clearance is the height of your antennas. This will help you make the decision to go under something at speed, or to slow down.

One way to establish your heights is to find a level spot and get a laser level and a tape measure. When you are towing a fifth wheel you are doing it from the comfort of your tow vehicle which does not reflect that mass behind you, and which can easily be six-plus feet higher than your head.

Use the Data Worksheet in the appendix to record your dimensions. It would also be handy to have the metric conversions, just in case. After you have taken the dimensions, consider making a plaque and attaching it to your dash.

Securing and Un-Securing Your Vehicle

It is very important that you have complete control of your vehicle at all times. The best time to take control is when you are starting or stopping. You should always have two means of control during the transition from being parked to driving: the parking brake and the foot brake, or the transmission and the foot brake.

When un-securing your vehicle, hold the foot brake, put the transmission in gear, and release the parking brake. Before starting to move, make a full, or 100 percent, brake application to check your brakes.

Also, if it is the first time you are starting out after hitching the trailer, check your trailer brakes. Manually engage the brake controller and pull forward to check the brakes.

When securing your vehicle, hold the foot brake with the minimum amount of pressure required to keep the rig from moving. Then apply the parking brake, shift into park (or neutral if you do not have park) and release the foot brake, ensuring the vehicle does not move.

Drive smart: Know your vehicle.

CHAPTER 3

Maneuvering Basics

You want me to put it where?

I was watching an interview with an Indy 500 racecar driver several years ago and he said, "Anybody can drive an Indy car at 200 m.p.h. in a straight line; it's when you need to turn that the problems start."

I think that statement is very appropriate to driving anything with wheels.

Technically there are two types of drivers: personal and commercial. But in actuality there is a third—a "professional" driver. Most people think of a professional driver as one who gets paid to drive. But one of the definitions of a professional is a person who does something with great skill.

My goal is to provide you with the tools you can apply to help you become a professional driver. That means professionalism developed through the ongoing awareness of driving larger vehicles, and the execution of unique driving techniques needed to become a safer and more confident driver.

I have heard many stories about tight situations people have experienced. Most of the time it's a lack of understanding of the dynamics of how your rig turns that make it a "tight situation" to begin with.

The key to completing a successful maneuver with any vehicle is to know how it turns. You need to know where its Pivot Point is. You need to understand what Off Tracking is and how it affects a turn. In addition, you need to know how much tail swing you have. By understanding these three factors you can then determine where to place the Pivot Point of the trailer to properly set up for a maneuver.

There is no magic formula for maneuvering a fifth wheel trailer. With the variety of tow vehicles and trailers every combination is slightly different.

As a driving instructor I find that most people do not understand how a basic vehicle turns, let alone what happens when you add a trailer. As with just about anything, to be good at it you need to understand the basics. Another thing I have found is that it is very helpful for the student to try the maneuver and then get out and watch it being done. If you have your co-pilot maneuver the rig while you are watching, this will give them a good opportunity to understand what you can or cannot see, and some of the challenges you face.

Definitions

Before I begin talking about maneuvering a fifth wheel I would like to start with the definitions for a basic vehicle. Let's take a look at each one and see the effect it has on maneuvering:

The **Pivot Point** is defined as the fixed point on a vehicle at which the vehicle rotates around in a turn. On a two-axle vehicle it is the center of the rear axle. This means that if an object, for example a tree, is located at the center of the rear axle or behind, you can turn toward the object and not hit it, (the rear of the vehicle will swing away from the object). If the object is ahead of the Pivot Point and you turn toward it, you *will* hit it.

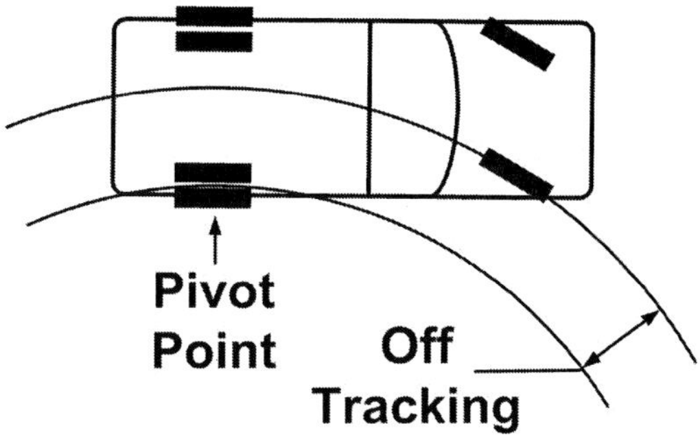

Off Tracking is the difference between the path of the front wheels and the rear wheels, during the course of a turn. This is what gets people in trouble when they turn a longer vehicle.

Tail Swing is the distance the body of the vehicle behind the pivot point moves in the opposite direction of the front when you turn.

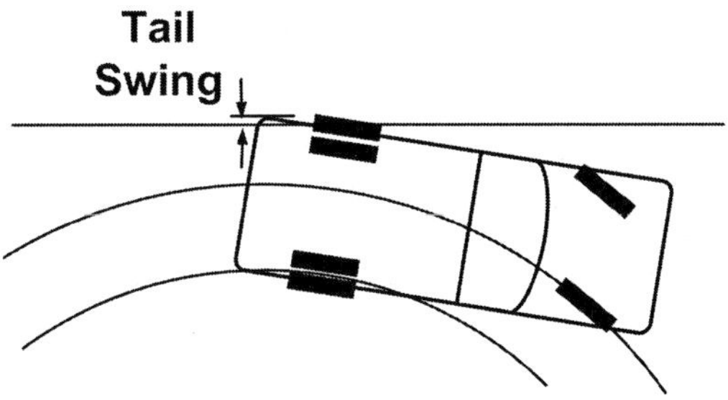

When you add a trailer, you are also adding an additional set of factors: a second Pivot Point, Off Tracking, and Tail Swing to the equation.

A conventional trailer will somewhat track around a corner. It does this because it is hitched to the rear of the tow vehicle, and when you turn, the rear of the tow vehicle swings the opposite direction of the turn, causing the trailer to follow a larger radius during the turn. The longer the trailer the more it will Off Track; the shorter the trailer the less Off Tracking.

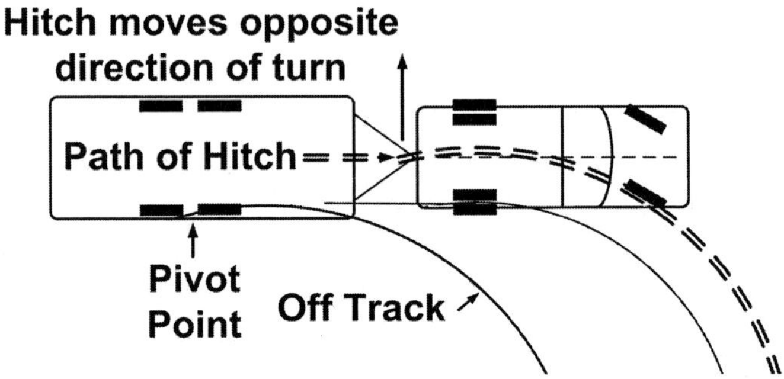

With a fifth wheel trailer the dynamics change notably. The King Pin, or hitch point, is generally just ahead of the center of the drive axle. This means that when you start turning, the trailer also starts turning in the same direction at the same time, which means the Off Tracking is greater, and increases the more you continue the turn.

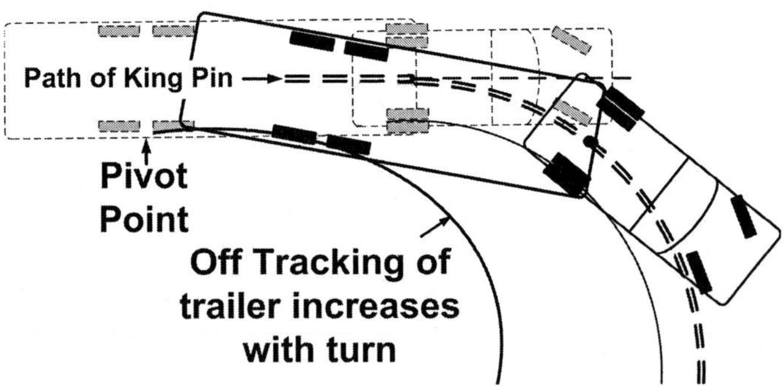

You have probably heard the term "**Jack Knife**" when referring to semi trucks. Jack-Knifing occurs when a turn is made too sharply, causing the tow vehicle and trailer to collide.

This applies to any trailer when you turn too sharply. With a fifth wheel trailer it can vary from hitting the cab on a short bed pick-up with the front of the trailer, to hitting the cab with the side of the trailer for a long bed pick-up that allows you to turn greater that 90 degrees.

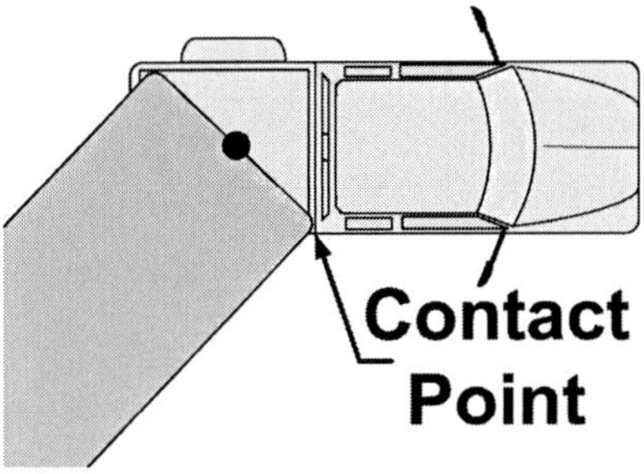

Short Bed

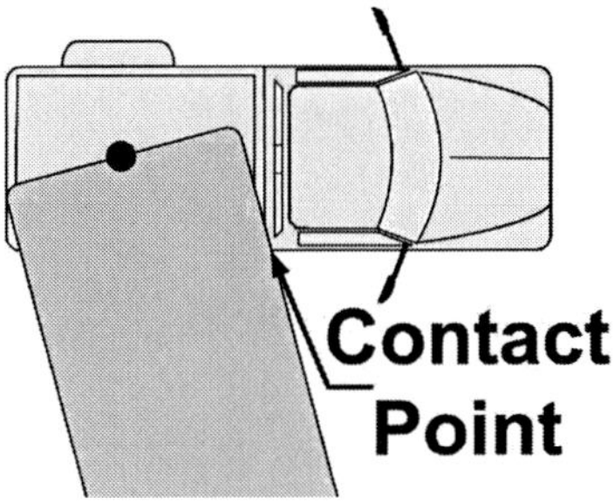

Long Bed

I should note here that for a short bed pick-up, the use of a sliding hitch assembly allows you to turn farther before jack-knifing occurs.

To help you maneuver you need to know where the Pivot Point of your trailer is. To do this, park your rig straight and then mark the Pivot Point with something that you can see in the mirrors—such as a cone on its side, a block of wood, etc. The Pivot Point for a single axle would be the center of the axle; a tandem axle would be the center between the axles; and a triple axle would be the center axle. Sitting in the driver's seat, look in the mirrors and look at your marks. Look along the line from where you are looking at the mirror and the marks on the ground… Is there something along that line of sight that you can see in the mirror to use as a reference? If not, try putting a mark on the front of the trailer.

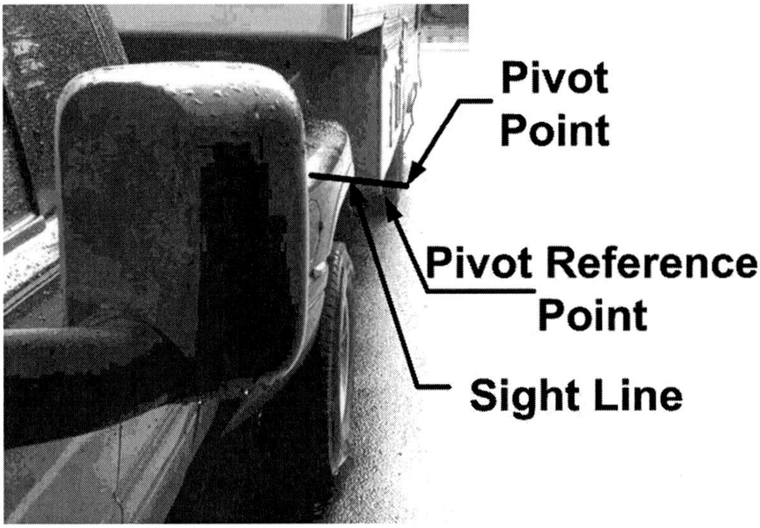

Once you have established these reference points you will have a guide to help you turn. When looking in the mirror if an obstruction lies below your pivot reference point, you have not reached it yet. When the obstruction is above your pivot reference point you have passed it and are free to turn. That's based on the obstruction being right alongside your trailer. Because your rig off-tracks, if it was two feet away from the object you may be able to start your turn six to eight feet sooner without contacting the obstruction.

Turn offset

You really don't need to know how much your rig off-tracks; you just need to know what it is and how it affects the way your rig turns.

There are some things you could do to help you understand how it affects turning… something as simple as going to a dirt or gravel lot where you will be able to see your tire tracks. Remember to take a rake with you to give yourself a clean palette to work with each time.

Or if you want to get more detailed, establish what I call "Turn Offsets." This is a method I developed to help someone understand how their rig turns and establish hard numbers to help them set up for a turn.

Let's take a look at how you can establish this information and how to use it.

This is where you will need to do some homework. I have included a Data Worksheet in the Appendix to record your findings. My suggestion is go to a large parking lot, like a mall, in the morning when traffic is light.

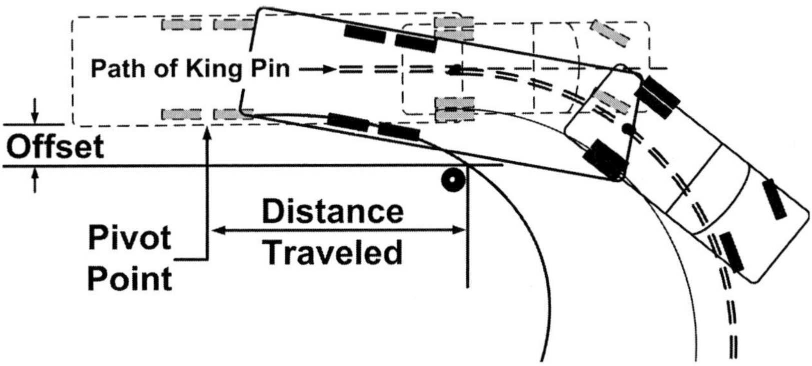

To establish your Turn Offsets, park your rig parallel to a line one foot away. Then mark the line adjacent to your Pivot Point. Now, turn the wheels full lock (as far as they will turn in the direction you want to go), in the direction of the line, and move forward until the pivot point of the trailer intersects the line. Then, measure the distance that you have traveled from the starting mark that you put on the line to the Pivot Point.

It doesn't hurt to take these measurements turning both left and right. This gives you an opportunity to see what it looks like in the mirrors (and not all vehicles turn the same in both directions).

Repeating this exercise at two, three, and four feet will give you a good indication of how your rig turns.

After you have gathered your Turn Offset and tail swing information, you will know what you need to do to properly get ready for a maneuver. The Setup is the most important part of a maneuver.

Setup

Setup is how you position your rig to start a maneuver after taking all of the above into consideration.

If you look at the three Setup examples you will see the same turn Setup from three different starting positions. On the left you see what it looks like when you start your turn when the rear of the trailer is at the obstruction. The middle view shows the turn starting when the Pivot Point of the trailer is adjacent to the obstruction. As you can see, the overall space required to complete the turn is shortened by the length of the trailer rear overhang. The turn on the right illustrates what can be done when the Turn Offset data is applied. By Setting Up farther away from the obstruction and starting to turn earlier, you would be able to turn into a much smaller lane or opening. Also, by knowing your tail swing you know at least how far to be from a wall or other objects before you start your turn. In traffic you will need to allow space in the lane on the opposite side from the direction that you are turning, for your tail to swing into.

Something I need to stress here is: Don't force a turn. If there is not enough room to make the maneuver, stop and wait for traffic to clear to complete your turn. And if it doesn't look like there is enough room to make the maneuver, *don't do it.*

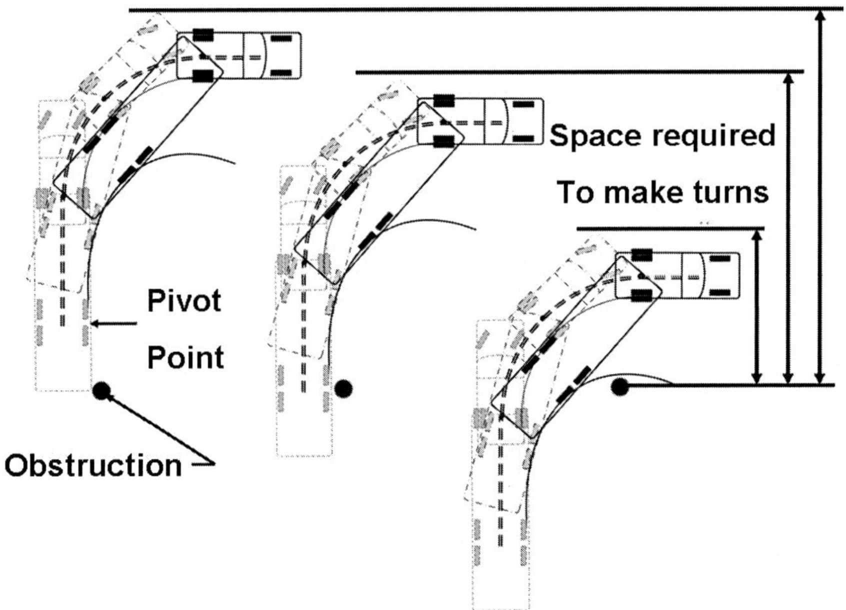

If you haven't realized it yet, what I am telling you is that you are actually *"Steering from the rear."* It's what you do when driving anything, but it is not apparent until you drive a longer vehicle.

Drive smart: Maneuver with skill.

CHAPTER 4

Backing Up

Unfortunately you can't always get a pull-through.

Backing a trailer can be a challenge. And backing a fifth wheel trailer is different from backing a conventional trailer—so much so that my recommendation is to forget anything you think you know about backing a trailer and approach it as if everything is new. Unfortunately backing a trailer does not come naturally to most people. For most of us it is a long, slow learning process. The challenge here is that, because of the variety of combinations of tow vehicles and trailers, they all react differently. With a short tow rig and long trailer the trailer will react much more slowly. The opposite is true when you have a long rig and short trailer; in this case, the trailer reacts more quickly.

In this chapter I will be describing several different techniques. What works for some does not necessarily work for others. It must be a right brain/left brain thing. Try all of these techniques to see what works best for you.

Backing to the left is generally easier than backing to the right. You have better visibility on the driver's side. Many campgrounds are laid out so that you back to the left into the sites for exactly this reason.

Mirrors are essential tools when backing a trailer. It is safer to use the mirrors, rather than opening the door to look or hanging out the window. A properly set and adjusted mirror will give you the best view when backing. If you are uncomfortable using your mirrors for backing you need to work on becoming comfortable with them. The goal is to keep the trailer wheels in sight of your mirrors at all times when backing.

Knowing where to start your turn is called Set Up. Remember the turning exercises that I covered in the basic maneuvering section in Chapter 3? By observing how much your trailer off tracks will give you a good feel on how you need to Set Up for a backing maneuver.

Before you start to back up, get out and walk the area first. Look at where you want to go and pick a target where you want the trailer wheels to go as you maneuver. Establish predetermined stop points, and then stop and check when you reach that predetermined point, and adjust as necessary. It is not unreasonable to pick several points along the way. Remember the Pivot Point of your trailer? That's the wheels of your trailer and that is what you want to use as your guide. Repeat this process as many times as needed. Also, be sure to look up as well. Those tree branches just love to reach out and grab things.

Start by pulling up straight; as you stop, turn the wheels on your tow vehicle in the opposite direction from where you want the trailer to go. This will get the trailer heading in the right direction when you start backing. This is sometimes called "Jacking" the trailer.

You want to back up at an idle speed—only use the throttle as necessary to keep you moving. Once the trailer starts to turn, you need to "catch up" with it. By this I mean turning the wheels back toward center (straight) until you "catch up" with the trailer and then steer, more or less, as needed, to keep the trailer going where you want it to go. By "catching up" with the trailer you will have reached the point where the angle between the truck and trailer remain the same as you back up. This is sometimes called "Chasing" the trailer.

Some people will tell you that, when chasing the trailer, put your hand on the bottom of the steering wheel so that when you turn the steering wheel the bottom is moving in the direction that you want the trailer to go. Others will tell you to hold your hand at the top of the steering wheel and steer the opposite direction.

Still others will tell you to watch your mirrors. To slow the turn down, turn your front wheels in the direction that you see the most trailer in the mirror. Example: If there is more of the trailer visible in the left mirror, you need to turn the wheels to the left, if you want to keep turning that direction, or to turn faster, turn the opposite way.

Both styles work well. I would say try them all and do whatever comes most naturally to you.

You'll want to keep your steering actions to a minimum, only steering enough to keep the trailer wheels on the projected path to your target.

As you are following the trailer back and you want the trailer to go in the opposite direction, turn the front wheels accordingly. Doing this will slow down the turn. However, the trailer will not start going in the opposite direction until the tow vehicle has passed through straight with the trailer. This is why keeping your turning angle to a minimum gives you more control when backing. The sharper the angle between the truck and trailer, the further you will travel before the trailer goes in the direction you want, and most of the time you will not have the extra room.

The tendency is to steer too much. If you let the angle between the trailer and the tow rig get too sharp you'll reach a point where you will not be able to recover as you back up. In some cases that is exactly what you may want to do… For example this type of maneuver should only be used for gross re-alignments followed by a pull up, or at the end of the maneuver for final positioning.

Don't be afraid to do a "Pull Up" if things are not working out. It is better to pull forward and fix the path early, before it gets to the point where you need to pull out and start over. It is much easier to fix the problem with a little forward movement than trying to catch up in reverse.

If possible have a spotter guide you. You'll need to be able to communicate either through hand signals or by using radios. Talk about it first so that you understand the signals. If you use hand signals have the spotter stand where they can be seen in the flat mirror and make sure the spotter makes big movements. To keep the driver's face visible in the flat mirror the spotter may need to move as you turn. You should always be able to see each other's face. Remember: G.O.A.L.: If something doesn't look right, *stop* and Get Out And Look.

I wish there was something magic to say here, but there is not. Becoming proficient at backing a fifth wheel trailer takes practice, so use every time you back your trailer as a learning experience. Something else you can do is to take every opportunity to watch someone else back a fifth wheel trailer. You can learn as much by watching as you can by doing.

The mantra is: Practice. Practice. Practice!

Before you start backing up turn off the radio, CB, etc. to eliminate distractions, open your window, and tap your electric horn, not the air, to warn people around you. This will also give others like you the chance to watch and learn.

Drive smart: Go back and read this one again.

CHAPTER 5

Driving

Boy, this thing is big.

Now let's take the information I have given you and apply it to going down the road and other real-life driving situations. There are many techniques that can help you become a safer, more confident driver. Some of the things covered in this chapter include: how to steer using reference points; how to drive in congested traffic in an urban downtown; how to use your transmission; and merging in traffic.

Steering

The steering technique that I teach is called Shuffle Steering. Relax the upper portion of your arms along your side and extend your lower arms straight out to where they touch the wheel. Don't reach for the top or outer edge.

The normal position for your hands on the steering wheel of a car are at 10 and 2 o'clock. When driving a pickup or special tow vehicle, the steering wheel may be larger or set flatter. If this is the case and you feel that you are reaching out too far, consider shifting your grip to the 8 and 4 o'clock positions. In most cases you will find this to be much more comfortable and you will still have full control.

The best way I can explain this is to have you do a little exercise. Hold your arms straight out, have someone push sideways, and try to resist. Then repeat with your upper arms at your side and only your lower arms out. This is much easier to resist and your arms will not tire as fast.

Your grip needs to be soft, like driving with eggs in your hands. This gives you much better control and also reduces fatigue. You turn by "shuffling the wheel" through your hands so that you always have both hands on the wheel. Never let it "free-wheel" when coming out of a corner. You can practice the Shuffle Steering technique when driving your car. If you feel you can't keep up with the steering wheel when Shuffle Steering, then slow down; you're probably taking the corner too fast anyway.

Never "spoke" the wheel (hanging onto the steering wheel spokes) and do not hang onto the bottom of the wheel, as this magnifies your hand movements, which gives you less leverage in an emergency. Never palm the wheel (spinning the wheel with an open hand) as you have no grip on the wheel, which means no positive control.

At this point let's talk about some things I call "Road Push" and "Wind Push." When driving down the road sometimes your rig will seem to have a mind of its own. It will take off in a direction that you weren't planning to go. Many roads have ruts, worn by trucks that generally have a different track width than your rig. What happens is that, unless you are perfectly centered, one tire or the other will want to drop into the rut, pushing you around. If this happens try moving to one side of the lane to see if you can find an area where things are in balance.

Another thing that can make the rig move around is the wind. I don't know how to describe it... it's just an instinctive feel. The body of a tow vehicle with air suspension will sometimes move around on its axels. If you feel that you are starting to wander around, you should begin looking at indicators such as trees, road conditions, etc., to see what is affecting the movement. If you are chasing the body you can find yourself wandering all over the road. The lesson here is that you need to learn to steer the wheels not the body.

Reference Points

Another problem some people have is maintaining a straight course and knowing where they are in relationship to the lane.

The best way to do this is to establish Reference Points. You probably already do this subconsciously. Without looking, can you tell me what those points are? When you go to the parking lot to establish your turn data, park with the driver's side of the trailer on a long line and see where that line intersects with the bottom of the windshield or hood. If there is no specific Reference Point, mark that spot with a piece of tape or sticky dots. Then, move the trailer, putting the line on the passenger side, and mark the windshield the same way. This will provide you with your limits. Your mind automatically tries to center things; by establishing these marks it will provide your subconscious with the necessary guidance to stay centered in your lane and maintain a straight course.

Note how the dots are centered in the lane.

For example, this is beneficial when you are driving on a dark rainy night, and you arrive at a narrow bridge where there is oncoming traffic. Just set your marks (Reference Points) and proceed because you will not be able to see anything else.

You also can use your marks on a bright, sunny day when the sun reflects off the windshield and all you see is one side of the road. The Reference Points will keep you on a safe path.

These Reference Points work fine when driving along straight or gently curving roads. Do you also remember Off Tracking and that you actually steer from the rear? As you drive along twisting roads, steering from the rear to keep your wheels on the road, observe where the center and "fog lines" are in relationship to your reference marks. (The fog line is the solid line on the right side of the road.) This becomes very helpful when driving at night.

Remember that you steer from the rear, so you must drive the front a lot further out than you think to keep the trailer wheels on the road. Also remember that Reference Points will be different for each driver.

Mirror: Friend or Foe?

Mirrors play a critical part in driving; they are helpful, of course, but they also can be your enemy. Larger mirrors, especially the truck-style ones on some of the special-made tow vehicles, are nice for seeing what is behind you, but they also block your view to the front. It is easy to loose sight of people, bicycles, small cars, telephone poles and the like, that seem to spring up behind them. If you have this style of mirrors, make sure that you look around them before you move and while driving.

Only thing moved was the camera.

Transmissions

"D" is for dummies. Most people put their transmission in Drive (D), and then just drive. That's not always the best thing to do in a larger rig. Most transmissions are programmed for economy and emissions, not performance. When you come to that hill, shift down one, or maybe two, gears as you proceed up the grade—before you start to lose speed. How many gears you shift up or down will vary from rig to rig; just be sure to keep an eye on your RPMs. You will find that in most cases you can climb the hill without much reduction in speed, and you may even get better fuel economy.

I am sure that you've heard the old adage that you go down a hill in the same gear you needed for going up the hill. You are much better using the engine as a brake rather than using your brakes alone. It is far safer going downhill at 15 to 20 m.p.h. in first gear and using your brakes sparingly, rather than 30 to 35 m.p.h. and using your brakes more often.

If your tow vehicle is equipped with a retarder, grade braking, or a tow haul function, the transmission is acting as a brake by restricting the transmission fluid. If you have one of these types of transmissions be sure to watch your transmission temperature, as it can rise rapidly during use.

Another very important thing to do when shifting from forward into reverse, or the other way around, is to pause or shift into neutral between forward and reverse to allow the drive train to relax before changing direction. With a column shift you do this automatically, but you should still pause momentarily in neutral. If you have one of those special-built tow vehicles with a keypad shifter you will need to shift into neutral and then into drive/reverse as needed. If you shift directly from one direction to the other with any movement you can twist off a drive shaft very easily.

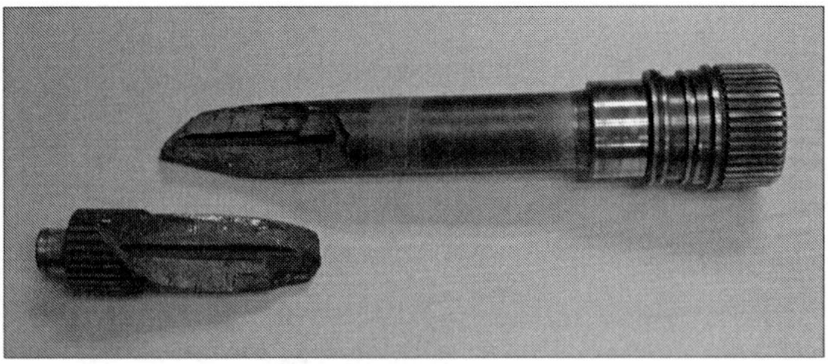

Twisting a shaft is what you don't want to do.

Advisory Signs

You see many advisory signs when driving. Speed limits can change frequently, depending on where you are, and, if you're driving your automobile, you may or may not slow down as much as a sign advises. When driving a large vehicle, however, slow down to the posted advisory speed, unless you have first-hand knowledge of the area and its exact situation. It is always better to err on the side of caution.

Merging

Merging and changing lanes can sometimes present a challenge. A larger vehicle cannot accelerate or decelerate as quickly as the general traffic. You need to maintain as much speed as possible when merging or changing lanes. This is where I will teach you the use of "polite intimidation" and what the "cost coefficient" is.

In normal automobile driving you just wait for a large enough space, turn your turn signal on, and move over. It is when traffic gets heavy that you might need to get a little more creative. Don't just turn your signal on and wait for an opening. If you do that, most of the time no one will let you in, and after a while people will ignore your signal.

When you need to make your changing move, first move over to the opposite side of your lane from the direction you want to go. Then, turn your signal on and move over quickly enough so that the move is noticeable. When you move away first, there is more room to make your intended move more noticeable. The key here is to not cross the line until you have an opening. As long as you stay in your lane, and don't cross the line out of your lane, you haven't violated anything. The movement generally will cause other drivers to back off, which opens a space for you to move into.

If this doesn't work, turn off your signal, wait a while, and then try again. Just remember to move back over in your lane.

As a last resort you can use the cost coefficient. Using your mirrors, pick the most expensive car in the line of traffic coming up from behind. Turn your signal on just as the selected vehicle reaches your rear corner and can still see your turn signal, and then make your side movement. This works best if you have signals on the side of your rig. And don't forget to thank the person who let you in. You can blink your lights or turn your flashers on for two to three cycles.

Downtown

Let's talk a little about driving in towns and cities. I know what you are thinking: I don't drive downtown. Well, have you ever taken a wrong turn? Since you are reading this to yourself, you can admit it.

Downtown streets are usually narrower than highways. In some cases the lanes are only eight feet wide. If you are pulling an eight-and-a-half-foot wide trailer you need to be very careful. If traffic is light, then just drive in your lane, but if traffic is heavy it is sometimes safer to straddle two lanes.

Turning in town is harder to explain than it is to understand. In general it is best to be in the outer lane of the turn, the lane with the largest radius, when making turns on multiple-lane roads. When driving in big cities things change somewhat. The radius of the turn lanes is much smaller than your rig is able to turn. If there are double turn lanes, make the turn from the lane on the outside of the turn. Don't confuse the outer lane of the turn with the outside lane, which is the curb lane.

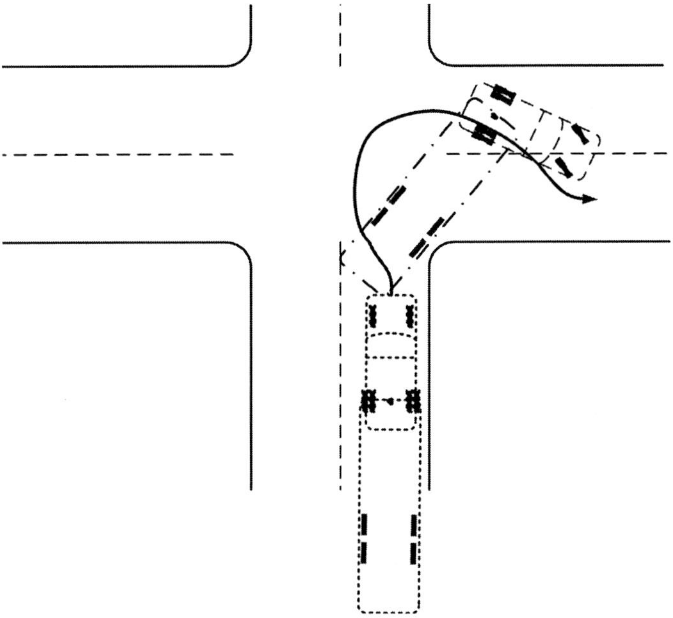

You need to block the curb lane.

When turning in an urban environment the most important thing to do is to be in control of the situation. Make your turns slowly and, if necessary, stop and let traffic clear. Other drivers may not like it, but when you slow down everyone around you must slow down as well and you have much more control over what happens.

When making a right turn you need to block the lane as you turn to keep someone from coming up alongside during your turn. You will need to swing wide and drive deep into the intersection as you Set Up. "Driving Deep" means that you may actually drive past the lane you are planning on turning into. Generally you do not want to cross the centerline, as this will give other drivers the impression that you are making a left turn. If you must cross over into the oncoming lane to make the turn, do it with caution and watch out for oncoming vehicles.

Making left-hand turns are much easier. Drive deep and, if necessary, swing wide. If you start turning too soon you take the risk of striking vehicles waiting to cross the intersection. Unfortunately most people don't understand what those stop bars on the pavement are for, and they quite often stop way past them, which makes turning more challenging.

Don't forget to check your side mirrors during the turn. You should, at a minimum, check both sides at the start, middle, and end of the turn so that you aren't surprised by cars or people who have no idea how much room it takes for your vehicle to turn. If there is a space, other vehicles, especially taxicabs, will fill it. You should also be checking your tail swing. Remember: when you are turning left you have much better visibility to your inside than you do on a right turn.

Don't force a turn, wait for traffic to clear.

Drive smart:
Proper planning prevents poor performance.

CHAPTER 6

The Art of Braking

"Whoa, Nellie!"

The braking technique that I teach drivers is "Feather Braking." To feather-brake you apply the brakes gently, come down on them firmly, and then slowly back off the pedal as you come to a stop. This will take the "jerk" out of the end of the stop. When this is done correctly you can even make a panic stop as smooth as silk.

The brakes on the tow vehicle and trailer are a critical element to safe towing.

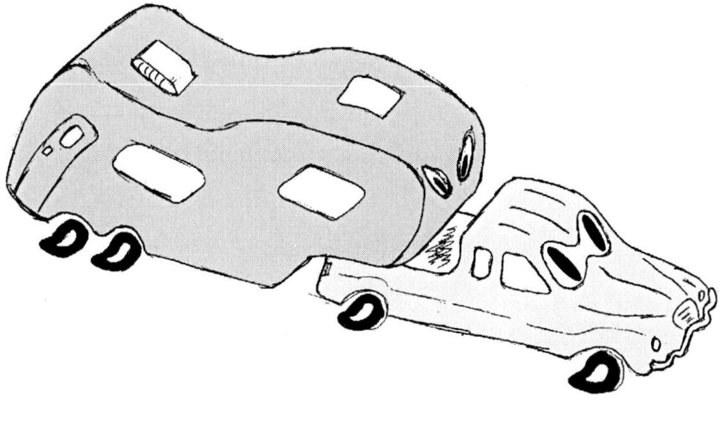

Have your trailer brakes, bearings and other components inspected at least once annually by a professional.

Do not use the tow vehicle's brakes to control excessive trailer sway—this will usually make it worse. Manually apply the trailer brakes to regain control.

When descending a steep incline, if it feels like the trailer is pushing the tow vehicle, reduce speed, down shift to a lower gear and use the manual override on the brake control to slow the trailer. Heavy use of the tow vehicle brakes can cause them to overheat and fade.

Most trailers have electric brakes; some will have hydraulic brakes. A brake controller mounted in the tow vehicle will activate both types. The brake controller sends an electrical current to the trailer brakes. Some types will send a radio signal to a controlled unit installed on the trailer. *(**Note**: Older brake controllers used to tie directly into the tow vehicle's hydraulic brake system. This type of connection interferes with ABS brake system operation.)*

There are two types of electric brake controllers: time-delay-activated and inertia-activated. Time-delay, or solid-state, controllers apply gradual voltage to the trailer brakes using a time-delay circuit. A pendulum circuit that applies gradual voltage to the trailer's brakes activates inertia, or pendulum, type controllers. Both types of brake controllers allow you to adjust the amount of braking power and they both have manual overrides that can be used to activate the trailer brakes without using the vehicle brakes. The override feature can be used when descending an incline, to assist in general slowing down, and to prevent premature brake wear on the tow vehicle. It is also helpful in regaining control if the trailer begins to sway or fishtail. ***Only a professional should do the installation of brake controllers and tow vehicle wiring.***

The electrical current sent to the trailer brakes energizes magnets, which are then attracted to a disc on the inside of the brake drum, similar to a disc brake. As the wheel turns, the actuator arm that the magnet is attached to is rotated, which acts as a cam that engages the brake shoes to the drum.

Some trailers will have what are called electric over hydraulic brakes. These types of systems can be disc or drum brakes. When the electrical current is sent to the trailer it activates a hydraulic pump, which supplies pressure to the brake assemblies.

It is important that you match the brake controller to the types of brakes that the trailer has to ensure proper braking. (***Note: Not all trailer axles have brakes and not all brake magnets draw the same current.***) Many of the new trucks come with an installed brake controller, which works with most brake systems. However, there are still some compatibility issues with some of the brake systems.

Don't forget to supplement your stopping power by using an auxiliary braking system if you have one. There are several types of auxiliary braking systems in use. Most commonly used on diesel engines are Compression Brakes, usually referred to as a "jake brake," and Exhaust Brakes, which are engine brakes that work off the exhaust back pressure. There are also Transmission Retarders, which can be used with either diesel or gas engines. In addition many of the newer transmissions have a setting that will downshift when needed to assist in slowing the vehicle.

You can also use the transmission by manually shifting down to a lower gear. When driving in heavy traffic it is a good idea to keep your auxiliary braking system on to give you that extra edge.

Learn how to use your auxiliary braking system. Many people tell me that when they turn on their auxiliary braking system, their rig starts shifting down and coming to a stop. If this is happening to you, the vehicle is driving you; you are not driving the vehicle. There is a definite point between acceleration and deceleration. With every vehicle that I have driven I've been able to find that point where you are not accelerating or decelerating. I call that point "floating the throttle."

The Braking Equation

When stopping a vehicle there are four phases that make up the stopping equation. These phases are:

1. **Perception Time**: The time it takes to recognize that you need to stop.
2. **Reaction Time**: The time it takes for you to apply the brakes.
3. **Brake Lag**: The time from when you apply pressure on the pedal to when the brakes start to engage. For hydraulic systems the time is negligible. I will note that for air brakes it can be up to a half-second.
4. **Stopping Distance**: the distance you travel after the brakes have engaged.

Of those four phases, you have control over only one phase. Your Reaction Time is *your* Reaction Time; there's not much you can do to improve it. Brake Lag—nothing you can do here either. Stopping distance is also a constant; your only control here is maintaining good tires and brakes. That leaves Perception Time, which is the one thing you do have control over.

Let me lay out a couple of scenarios. If you are traveling at 55 m.p.h., which is about 80 feet per second, it takes you three

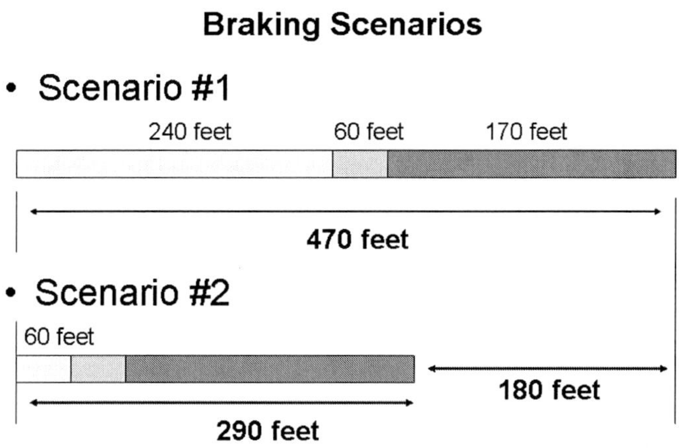

seconds to perceive a problem. You have traveled about 240 feet before you start to react.

Your Reaction Time, about three-fourths of a second, will take you another 60 feet. So far you have traveled 300 feet and you haven't started to stop yet. That's the length of a football field. With a nominal stopping distance of 170 feet you will have traveled a total of 470 feet before you have completed your stop.

Okay, now let's look at the same scenario using the Perception Time of a trained driver. This is about three-fourths of a second, which means the driver would only travel 60 feet before starting to react. That is 180 feet less, which means you will stop 180 feet sooner.

Stop and think about that for a moment… 180 feet is more than half the length of a football field. This means that you would stop in 290 feet, versus 470 feet. I can lay out all sorts of scenarios, but three to five seconds of Perception Time is not unrealistic for the untrained driver.

Drive smart: Brake smartly.

CHAPTER 7

Mind Set

Driving is 10 percent physical and 90 percent mental.

So what can you do to improve your Perception Time? This is where I am going to introduce you to "Perception Driving" and the "principles of smart driving," sometimes called "space cushion driving."

The National Safety Council reports that an average of one out of every four drivers is involved in a reportable accident every year. Tire marks at the scenes indicate that the trouble was realized, but often too late. In most cases the driver had robbed him- or herself of sufficient space or time to react to the hazard by following too closely. The closer you follow, the more you focus on the vehicle in front of you. It's like wearing blinders and you don't see what is developing around you.

Perception Driving

To drive safely you need to perceive, predict, and perform. You must first perceive the potential trouble. This means seeing the hazard both physically (10 percent), and then understanding what it means, mentally (90 percent), to the driving situation at hand. Only then can you decide what action is necessary in order to avoid being involved in a collision. Then you must perform such action in time, before it is too late.

The Principles of Smart Driving

Okay, so how do you achieve this? You learn to use the following principles.

• **Aim high in steering.** While driving, your main consideration is to find a safe path for your vehicle to travel. It's the same basic principle for any activity. For example, when you walk at 3–4 m.p.h., you look approximately 25 feet ahead, and your stopping distance is about 2 feet. As the speed increases the distance you need to be aware of increases many times over. Set your sights high. When driving in the city, look at least one block ahead, and on the highway look at least a quarter of a mile ahead. A rule of thumb is to set your sights to where you will be in about fifteen seconds. At first try counting this out just like following distance. You will be surprised at how your eye can deceive you when it comes to measuring distance, especially at highway speeds.

If you are not looking far enough ahead you are "low aim sighting." Some indications of low aim sighting are:

1. Hugging one side of the road.
2. Swinging wide to avoid parked vehicles.
3. Over-steering on turns, making wide unnecessary sweeps.
4. Unnecessarily swinging the opposite direction before making a turn.

These actions indicate that your eyes are leading your wheels.

You also need to be careful not to establish a fixed stare straight ahead, which leads to the next principle…

- **Get the big picture.** What exactly is the big picture? Your traffic picture is the sum total of every conflict that can be perceived. It is not only what you see, but also what you *should* see. Remember this is a constantly changing picture. Earlier I talked about aiming high; now that needs to be expanded. In town look at least one block ahead and from sidewalk to sidewalk. On the highway look at least a quarter-mile ahead and from fence to fence. Don't forget to include what is behind you as you scan your surroundings. Remember, 30 percent of hazards come from the rear. Your big picture should contain stationary objects, such as traffic lights and signs, lamp poles, parked vehicles and obstructions, as well as moving objects—pedestrians, people in vehicles, bicycles and motorcycles. Basically, anything that can move may become a hazard. You also need to observe instructions, warnings and traffic control devices. Being aware of all these things gives you an opportunity to anticipate the actions of others.

- **Keep your eyes moving.** The only way you can satisfactorily perform the first two principles is to keep your eyes moving. Your big picture is constantly changing so you continually need to scan the surrounding area, as well as your mirrors, to update your data input. You should make a complete scanning cycle about every eight seconds, even when you are stopped.

Okay, now that I have told you where to look, how to look and what to look for, what do you do with that information? Your eyes are only part of this equation; you will need to use your mind to interpret the data. If you look at a picture you may not see the subtle details. As you keep your eyes moving you need to identify each potential hazard, what the hazard may do, and recognize what your response should be.

An example of an individual hazard would be a car approaching a crossroad, coming to a stop sign. Is the car slowing down or is it coming too fast? Do you do nothing, slow down, stop, or take evasive action? As you identify each hazard, prioritize it in the order you need to address it.

At first this seems like too much to do, but after a while you can do it subconsciously to the point where it becomes an automatic reaction. I start my students out by asking them to tell me what they see and what the potential hazard is. There is no way you can say out loud what your mind is thinking, but this is a good exercise for getting the thought process started. Most of this you are already doing; you'll just need to refine it and adjust it to a larger vehicle.

• **Leave yourself an out.** The first thing you need to do to ensure yourself an out is to maintain a safe following distance. With all that data I have just asked you to gather and evaluate, you'll need some time and space to do something with it. I am sure that you all remember the two-second rule, or one-car length for every 10 m.p.h. following distance that you were taught when you learned to drive. Well, that's fine for a car, not an RV. The larger the vehicle, the more distance you need.

The basic rule of thumb for following distance is one second for every 10 feet of vehicle length for speeds up to 40 m.p.h. For speeds over 40 m.p.h., add one second. I would recommend that if you are over a ten-foot increment, round up to the next break. Using this rule the recommended minimum following distance for a 40-foot overall vehicle length would be four seconds on dry pavement for speeds up to 40 m.p.h. For speeds 40 m.p.h. and above, this would be expanded to five seconds. These times should be further expanded to suit conditions such as wet pavement, mud, or snow and ice. Adding an additional second for each is not unreasonable.

I know what you are thinking here: that there is no way you can maintain that much following distance. I agree; you probably won't be able to maintain the proper following distance all the time, but try your best. You might be surprised at how often you can achieve this. Maintaining a safe following distance will give you time and enough maneuvering room to avoid hazards. To measure following distance, note when the vehicle ahead of you passes a mark on the road then start counting... one thousand and one, one thousand and two, etc., until you reach that mark. In addition, don't let your cruise control set you up by bringing you too close behind someone.

You also need to leave yourself an out when stopped. A rule of thumb is to stop so you can still see the rear wheels of the vehicle ahead of you. This will give you sufficient room to maneuver if traffic stalls. Also, when going through an intersection, check to be sure there is enough room for your entire rig to clear the intersection when you stop. This can sometimes be very difficult because people will drive around you and fill the hole. But if you pull up and do not clear the intersection, you are the one who will get the ticket, not them.

- **Make sure they see you.** Drive with your lights on. When approaching a potential conflict, make eye contact if possible. Observe the driver. Is the driver looking at you? Is there a blank look on the person's face? Is the driver looking around as if searching for an address? Is the vehicle traveling faster than the rest of the traffic? And is there a place for it to pull into? Can you even see in the other car's window? You may need to flash your lights, or gently honk your horn. It is better to try to make contact early on than waiting till the last second when you lose your time and space to maneuver. Waiting too long may even cause the incident.

- **Always be prepared to yield.** Even though you may have done everything correctly, others might not have. Even if you do make eye contact with the other person, and you have the legal right of way, the driver may not give it to you. A good example of this is when cars merge on the freeway. Instead of yielding they think that if they have their turn signal on (if they use it at all), that they have the right of way. Other challenging areas are intersections. When approaching an intersection watch the light. When did it change last? If it was green when you first saw it, consider it a stale green light. Look for things like the pedestrian crossing lights and cars creeping into the intersection. You need to proceed with caution. You may even want to lift your foot off the accelerator and cover the brake, which will reduce your overall stopping distance. When driving along a street, watch the vehicles parked alongside the street. If they just pulled in, you can bet they will open their door in front of you. Watch for the exhaust that would indicate a running engine or the telltale signs of taillights coming on, as if the driver is putting it in gear to get ready to pull out. Expect the unexpected. Be proactive not reactive.

• **Drive in a manner in which *you* control the outcome.** We have now arrived at the last of the principles. None of the previous principles are any good if you do not have the right attitude. Do a "Check up from the Neck up." As I wrote earlier, you need to perceive, predict and perform. If your mind is not in the right state, you become reactive and you let others control you. Be cautious about others yet confident in your abilities. In other words, ***be proactive not reactive.***

Learn to accept what the other driver will do. It works against you if you get upset. Maintain your composure and you will control the outcome.

Drive smart: Keep your head in the game.

CHAPTER 8

Homework

You thought you could get out of this easily, didn't you?

I have now provided you with all the attributes you need to learn and master. So how do you master them? Here is where you get a homework assignment. The best way I have found is to think out loud when driving. Your brain works much faster than your mouth, but you need to start somewhere. Begin by describing what you see and where you see it. Then, evaluate what the potential hazards are and figure out your course(s) of action. I would suggest doing this while you are driving by yourself; otherwise it will drive your passenger nuts.

Practice: Backing, Shuffle Steering, Feather Braking, and Smart Driving.

I have created a data worksheet and placed it in the appendix for you to record your turning information, along with some other useful data. Do not forget to convert the measurements to metric as well. This could come in very handy if you go to Canada or Mexico.

I also recommend learning the weight by wheel or wheel group, which is helpful for proper loading and tire inflation. You can go to a public scale or stop at a weigh station along the highway when it is closed; some states leave them accessible. Most will have a visible scale readout, or a remote readout that you can view.

Drive smart. ***Write this one hundred times on the blackboard. (Sorry, I just had to say it.)***

CHAPTER 9

In Closing

I encourage you to seriously study, practice and attain the confidence to become a "professional" driver.

My main objective in writing this book is to provide you with the tools to help you have better control and become a safer driver, just like a professional. But I will confess that many of the techniques I have covered are also designed for passenger comfort. I know what you're thinking—"I don't carry passengers like a bus driver." *Well, remember that you usually have a passenger, and if you make them uncomfortable it can make for some cold nights.*

Drive smart: Enjoy the journey by towing your fifth wheel trailer like a pro!

APPENDIX 1

Truck & Trailer Selection Work Sheet:

Trailer Information:

________ GVWR
________ UVW
________ HW (brochure)
________ HW (20% GVWR)

Net Truck Payload:

________ Passengers
________ Cargo
________ Hitch
+ ________ HW
= ________ Net Payload

Truck Data:

________ MP
________ MLTWR
________ GVWR
________ GCWR

Calculated Curb Weight:

________ GVWR
- ________ MP
= ________ Curb Weight

Calculated Gross Vehicle Weight:

________ CW
________ NP
________ Options
+ ________ Accessories
= ________ Est. GVW

Finial Calculation:

________ GVW
- ________ HW
= ________ Net GVW
+ ________ Trailer GVWR
= ________ GCW

(#Passengers X 150 lbs; Water = 8.3lbs/gal; Gas = 5.6lbs/gal; Diesel = 6.8lbs/gal; Propane = 4.2lbs/gal)

APPENDIX 2

Data Worksheet

Height:

Hard _______ ft /_______ m

Soft _______ ft /_______ m

(1"=0.0254M)

Weight:

	Tow Rig Front	Tow Rig Rear	Trailer			
Right	_____	______	______			
Left	_____	______	______			
Total	_____	______	______	= _______	lb/_______	kg

(1#=0.4535kg)

Tail swing ___________________

Turn Off-Set:

@_____feet _____________________

@_____feet _____________________

@_____feet _____________________

@_____feet _____________________

Drive Smart Publications

Also available from Drive Smart Publications:

RAMBLING BY RV THROUGH
ALASKA & YUKON TERRITORY by Nyla Walsh

This is not your "typical" Travel Log on driving to Alaska and the Yukon Territory. Instead, you will travel along with Nyla and her husband Lorrin as they hit the highway north. As you read about their adventures you just might fall in love with traveling the highways of The Great Land.

Between the covers you will find: Adventures, Hints, Stories, History, Recipes, and a few laughs. For everyone who has ever been to Alaska, wants to go, or just enjoys armchair traveling, this book is for you.

$16.95 + $2.00 shipping and handling

DRIVE YOUR MOTORHOME
LIKE A PRO by Lorrin Walsh

A complete guide to professional driving techniques for beginners to experienced drivers.

$12.95 + $2.00 shipping and handling

Available at:

rvdrivesmart.com

or mail to:

Drive Smart Publications
PO Box 3690
Silverdale, WA 98383-3690

Order these RV publications for you and your traveling friends.

Lorrin Walsh first got involved with RVs in the early sixties when his parents bought a 13-foot camp trailer, their first of several. He started pulling trailers as soon as he got his learners permit, even before he got his drivers license. After he married he purchased his own travel trailer. He later migrated to motorhomes, but still pulls trailers for fun and some times for work.

A few years ago, after retirement from his job as a quality insurance inspector, Lorrin went to work for Gray Line of Seattle* as a driver/guide, just to get out of the house. After a couple of years Gray Line asked him to become a driving instructor.

The more training he did the more he realized how the information he gained from his almost 50 years of RV experience and what he taught as a driving instructor, would be helpful to anyone who pulls or drives an RV.

He decided to take this experience and put it in book to give drivers, new and old, the tools to help them become more confident and safer drivers.